sew Penguins, Puppies, Porcupines...oh my!

Kim Schaefer

39 BABY ANIMALS · QUILTS, BIBS, BLANKIES & MORE!

C&T PUBLISHING

Text copyright © 2021 by Kim Schaefer

Photography and artwork copyright © 2021 by C&T Publishing, Inc.

Publisher: Amy Barrett-Daffin

Creative Director: Gailen Runge

Acquisitions Editor: Roxane Cerda

Managing Editor: Liz Aneloski

Editor: Karla Menaugh

Technical Editor: Helen Frost

Cover/Book Designer: April Mostek

Production Coordinator: Tim Manibusan

Production Editor: Jennifer Warren

Illustrator: Mary E. Flynn

Photography Assistant: Gabriel Martinez

Photography by Lauren Herberg of C&T Publishing, Inc., unless otherwise noted

Published by C&T Publishing, Inc., P.O. Box 1456, Lafayette, CA 94549

Library of Congress Cataloging-in-Publication Data

Names: Schaefer, Kim, 1960- author.

Title: Sew penguins, puppies, porcupines... oh my! : 39 baby animals; quilts, bibs, blankies & more! / Kim Schaefer.

Description: Lafayette : C&T Publishing, 2021.

Identifiers: LCCN 2021032832 | ISBN 9781644031414 (trade paperback) | ISBN 9781644031421 (ebook)

Subjects: LCSH: Appliqué--Patterns. | Quilting--Patterns. | Animals in art. | Infants' clothing.

Classification: LCC TT779 .S334 2021 | DDC 746.44/5--dc23

LC record available at https://lccn.loc.gov/2021032832

Printed in the USA

10 9 8 7 6 5 4 3 2 1

ACKNOWLEDGMENTS

Special thanks to the following people:

Everyone at C&T Publishing for their continued support and encouragement.

Helen Frost, my technical editor at C&T Publishing, for once again checking and rechecking the accuracy of my work. Helen and I have worked together longer than I care to mention. I not only consider her the best technical editor ever but a friend as well. I am so grateful for all you do.

Susan Lawson of Seamingly Slawson Quilts, for her incredible longarm quilting. I am so happy to have found you. Your quilting is amazing.

My husband, Gary, for everything you do for me.

Special thanks to my daughter-in-law, Brittany Schaefer. Britt was a huge help in finding ready-made products for this book, including the diaper stackers, bibs, onesies, and diaper covers. Britt also gave us the gift of grandchild number fourteen, baby Kora Louise Schaefer. Baby Kora was a huge bright spot in the year 2020. I guess I should thank my son Max Schaefer for the gift of Kora as well. Apparently, he had a little to do with it.

Contents

PROJECTS

ZOO BABIES COLLECTION, 9

*Lion Cub, Monkey, Flamingo, Hippo, Penguin,
Elephant, Giraffe, Rhino, Tiger Cub*

WOODLAND BABIES COLLECTION, 27

Fox Pup, Raccoon, Owl, Skunk, Squirrel

 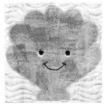    

Introduction

There is nothing quite like the joy and excitement that the arrival of a new baby brings, and no better way to celebrate the occasion than with a special gift that is handmade with love.

This book contains five collections of baby animals in 6″ blocks, including Northwoods, zoo, woodland, farm, and underwater baby animals. Each collection has a crib quilt and coordinating accessories. There are security blankies, bibs, diaper stackers, onesies, burp cloths, diaper covers, bench pillows, soft pictures, and a single framed block.

I hope that in the following pages you will find the perfect gift idea to welcome your new little one with love.

General Instructions

YARDAGE AND FABRIC REQUIREMENTS

I have given yardage and fabric requirements for each project. Use scraps for the baby animals or purchase ⅛- or ¼-yard cuts if your scrap bag is empty. All the projects are constructed using cotton fabrics. The cotton fabric amounts are based on a usable width of 42″. Fusible web amounts are based on a width of 17″.

ROTARY CUTTING

I recommend that you cut all the fabrics used in the blocks, borders, and bindings with a rotary cutter, an acrylic ruler, and a cutting mat. Trim the blocks and borders with these tools as well.

PIECING

All piecing measurements include ¼″ seam allowances. If you sew an accurate ¼″ seam, you will succeed! My biggest and best quiltmaking tip is to learn to sew an accurate ¼″ seam.

PRESSING

For cotton fabrics, press seams to one side, preferably toward the darker fabric. Press flat and avoid sliding the iron over the pieces, which can distort and stretch them. When you join two seamed sections, press the seams in opposite directions so you can nest the seams and reduce bulk.

APPLIQUÉ

All appliqué instructions are for paper-backed fusible web with machine appliqué. A lightweight paper-backed fusible web works best. Choose your favorite fusible web and follow the manufacturer's directions.

General Appliqué Instructions

1. Trace all parts of the appliqué design on the paper side of the fusible web. Trace each layer of the design separately. Some pieces are cut as connected shapes, shown with dotted lines on the patterns. Whenever 2 shapes in the design butt together, overlap them by about ⅛″ to help prevent the potential of a gap between them. When tracing the shapes, extend the underlapped edge ⅛″ beyond the drawn edge in the pattern. Write the pattern letter or number on each traced shape. *Note:* If a piece doesn't have a number, it is because that piece is a continuation of another piece, such as the ears being part of the head piece.

2. Cut around the traced appliqué shapes, leaving a ¼″ margin around each piece.

3. Iron each fusible web shape to the wrong side of the appropriate fabric, following the manufacturer's instructions for fusing. I don't worry about the grainline when placing the pieces. Cut on the traced lines and peel off the paper backing. A thin layer of fusible web will remain on the wrong side of the fabric. This layer will adhere the appliqué pieces to the backgrounds.

4. Position the pieces on the backgrounds. Press to fuse them in place.

5. Machine stitch around the appliqué pieces using a zigzag, satin, or blanket stitch. Stitch any other lines on the patterns to add detail. The dashed lines on the patterns show the suggested stitching lines.

6. Facial features are shown with solid lines. Use machine stitching or hand embroidery to bring life and personality to the animals. Eyes can be separate appliquéd pieces or inked in with a permanent fabric marker, such as Pigma Micron pens.

PUTTING IT ALL TOGETHER

When all the pieces are completed for a project, lay them out on the floor or, if you are lucky enough to have one, a design wall. Arrange and rearrange the pieces until you are happy with the overall look. Each project has specific directions as well as diagrams and photos for assembly.

LAYERING THE QUILT

Cut the batting and backing pieces 4″–5″ larger than the quilt top. Place the pressed backing on the bottom, right side down. Place the batting over the backing and the quilt top on top, right side up. Make sure that all the layers are flat and smooth and that the quilt top is centered over the batting and backing. Pin or baste the quilt.

NOTE: *If you are going to have your quilt quilted by a longarm quilter, contact them for specific batting and backing requirements, as they may differ from the instructions above.*

QUILTING

Quilting is a personal choice; you may prefer hand or machine quilting. My favorite method is to send the quilt top to a longarm quilter. This method keeps my number of unfinished tops low and the number of finished quilts high.

BINDING

The amounts for binding allow for 2″ strips cut on the straight grain. I usually use the same fabric for the backing and the binding. It is a good way to use leftover fabric. Cut the binding strips on either the crosswise or lengthwise grain of the leftover fabric, whichever will yield the longest strips.

Rounded Corners

The security blankies are made with rounded corners and feature a wider, bias-cut binding. While you could make the blankies with square corners, it's nice to round them off for a professional finish.

Zoo Babies Collection

BRING THE EXCITEMENT AND FUN OF THE ZOO INTO THE NURSERY WITH THE ZOO BABIES COLLECTION. THE COLLECTION INCLUDES A CRIB QUILT, SECURITY BLANKIE, ONESIE, BURP CLOTH, AND TWO BIBS.

Zoo Babies Crib Quilt

Finished block: 6″ × 6″ • **Finished quilt:** 30½″ × 30½″

Made by Kim Schaefer, quilted by Susan Lawson of Seamingly Slawson Quilts

MATERIALS

- ½ yard of white-on-white for appliqué block backgrounds
- ¾ yard total of assorted brights for border

- Scraps:

  3 oranges for lion mane and tail, flamingo legs, penguin beak and feet, giraffe horns, and tiger body

  4 yellows for lion body, monkey banana and peel, and giraffe body

  3 white-on-whites for lion mouth, monkey mouth, hippo teeth, penguin tummy, rhino horn, and tiger face and tummy

  4 blues for monkey body, tummy, and feet; and rhino body and feet

  1 brown for monkey tree branch

  1 green for monkey tree leaves

  4 pinks for flamingo body, wing, and beak; rhino and monkey ears; and hippo and elephant cheeks

  2 teals for hippo body, ears, and feet

  2 purples for elephant body, ears, feet, and tail

  1 gold for giraffe spots

  1 black for lion eyes, whiskers, and nose; monkey eyes and nose; flamingo eye and beak; hippo eyes; penguin body; elephant, giraffe, and rhino eyes; and tiger eyes, nose, and stripes

- 34″ × 34″ batting
- 1⅜ yards for backing and binding
- 1¾ yards of paper-backed fusible web
- Assorted threads for appliqué

CUTTING

White-on-white
- Cut 9 squares 6½″ × 6½″ for the appliqué block backgrounds.

Assorted brights
- Cut 16 squares 6½″ × 6½″ for the borders.

APPLIQUÉING

Refer to Appliqué (page 7) for detailed appliqué instructions.

1. Trace and prepare the pieces for each of these zoo babies: lion, monkey, flamingo, hippo, penguin, elephant, giraffe, rhino, and tiger (pages 18–26).

2. Appliqué the pieces for each zoo baby to a background square.

Block A: Lion cub

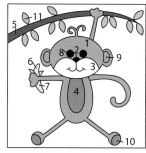
Block B: Baby monkey

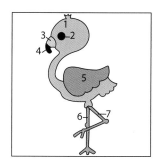
Block C: Baby flamingo

Block D: Baby hippo

Block E: Baby penguin

Block F: Baby elephant

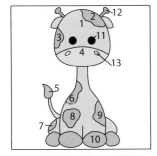

Block G: Baby giraffe

Block H: Baby rhino

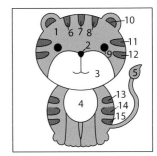

Block I: Tiger cub

PUTTING IT ALL TOGETHER

Refer to the diagram below.

1. Arrange and sew the blocks in 5 rows of 5 blocks each. Press.

2. Sew together the rows. Press.

FINISHING

1. Layer the quilt top with the batting and backing. Baste or pin.

2. Quilt as desired and bind.

Putting it all together

Baby Hippo Security Blankie

Finished blankie: 18″ × 18″

Made by
Kim Schaefer

MATERIALS

- ⅝ yard of blue minky for blankie front and back
- ½ yard of blue flannel for binding
- Scraps:

1 medium blue for hippo	1 pink for ears and cheeks
1 teal for feet	1 black for eyes
	1 white for teeth

- ¼ yard of paper-backed fusible web
- Template plastic
- Assorted threads for appliqué

CUTTING

Blue minky
- Cut 2 squares 18″ × 18″ for the blankie front and back.

Blue flannel
- Cut 3 bias strips 2¾″ wide for the binding.

Template plastic
- Trace and cut the corner pattern (above right). Place the template on the corners of the minky squares and trim the corners.

Cut blankie corners.

APPLIQUÉING

Refer to Appliqué (page 7) for detailed appliqué instructions.

1. Trace and prepare the pieces for the baby hippo (page 21).

2. Appliqué the baby hippo pieces to the blankie front.

PUTTING IT ALL TOGETHER

1. Sew the 2¾″-wide flannel strips together end to end to make a 74″ strip for the binding.

2. Fold the flannel binding strip in half lengthwise with wrong sides together and press flat.

3. Place the blankie front and back with wrong sides together.

4. Fold under the beginning end of the binding. Pin and sew the binding to the front of the blankie with the raw edges together and using a ¼″ seam. Overlap the ends and trim the excess. Finish stitching in place.

5. Turn the folded edge of the binding to the back of the blankie and hand stitch in place.

Security Blankie Corner

Baby Flamingo Bib

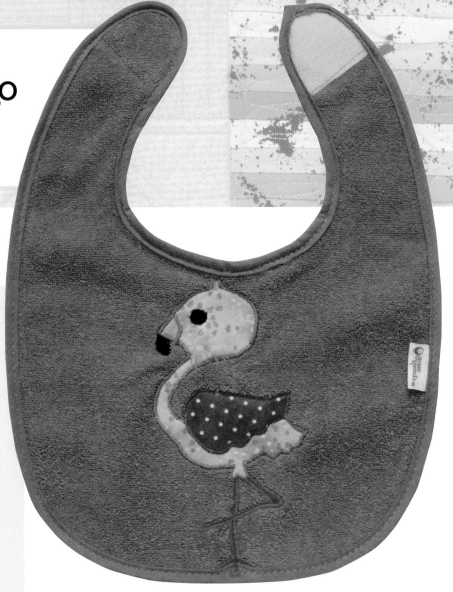

MATERIALS

- 1 pink ready-made bib

- Scraps:

    3 pinks for flamingo body, wing, and beak

    1 black for eye and beak

    1 orange for legs

- ¼ yard of paper-backed fusible web
- Assorted threads for appliqué

APPLIQUÉING

Refer to Appliqué (page 7) for detailed appliqué instructions.

1. Trace and prepare the pieces for the baby flamingo (page 20).

2. Appliqué the baby flamingo pieces to the bib.

Putting it all together

Lion Cub Bib

MATERIALS

· 1 yellow ready-made bib

· Scraps:

  1 yellow for lion body

  1 orange for mane, ears, and tail

  1 black for eyes, nose, and whiskers

  1 white for face

· ¼ yard of paper-backed fusible web

· Assorted threads for appliqué

APPLIQUÉING

Refer to Appliqué (page 7) for detailed appliqué instructions.

1. Trace and prepare the pieces for the lion cub (page 18).

2. Appliqué the lion cub pieces to the bib.

Putting it all together

Baby Elephant Onesie

MATERIALS

• 1 white ready-made onesie

• Scraps:

  1 dark purple for elephant body

  1 light purple for ears and feet

  1 pink for cheeks

  1 black for eyes

• ¼ yard of paper-backed fusible web

• Assorted threads for appliqué

APPLIQUÉING

Refer to Appliqué (page 7) for detailed appliqué instructions.

1. Trace and prepare the pieces for the baby elephant (page 23).

2. Appliqué the baby elephant pieces to the onesie.

Putting it all together

Baby Giraffe Burp Cloth

MATERIALS

· 1 ready-made burp cloth

· Scraps:

  2 yellows for giraffe body and mouth

  1 gold for spots

  1 orange for horns

  1 black for eyes and nostrils

· ¼ yard of paper-backed fusible web

· Assorted threads for appliqué

APPLIQUÉING

Refer to Appliqué (page 7) for detailed appliqué instructions.

1. Trace and prepare the pieces for the baby giraffe (page 24).

2. Appliqué the baby giraffe pieces to the burp cloth.

Putting it all together

Zoo Babies Patterns

LION CUB

· Cut 1 each of pattern pieces 1–6.

· Cut 2 of pattern piece 7.

· Cut 1 and 1 reverse each of pattern pieces 8, 9, and 10.

BABY MONKEY

- Cut 1 each of pattern pieces 1–7.

- Cut 2 of pattern piece 8.

- Cut 1 and 1 reverse each of pattern pieces 9 and 10.

- Cut 11 of pattern piece 11.

BABY FLAMINGO

· Cut 1 each of pattern pieces 1–7.

BABY HIPPO

· Cut 1 of pattern piece 1.

· Cut 2 of pattern piece 2.

· Cut 1 and 1 reverse each of pattern pieces 3–7.

BABY PENGUIN

- Cut 1 of pattern pieces 1–3.

- Cut 1 and 1 reverse each of pattern piece 4.

BABY ELEPHANT

· Cut 1 each of pattern pieces 1–3.

· Cut 2 each of pattern pieces 4 and 5.

· Cut 1 and 1 reverse each of pattern pieces 6–8.

BABY GIRAFFE

- Cut 1 each of pattern pieces 1–10.

- Cut 2 of pattern piece 11.

- Cut 1 and 1 reverse each of pattern pieces 12 and 13.

BABY RHINO

- Cut 1 each of pattern pieces 1 and 2.

- Cut 2 each of pattern pieces 3 and 4.

- Cut 6 of pattern piece 5.

- Cut 1 and 1 reverse each of pattern pieces 6 and 7.

TIGER CUB

- Cut 1 each of pattern pieces 1–8.

- Cut 2 of pattern piece 9.

- Cut 1 and 1 reverse each of pattern pieces 10–15.

Woodland Babies Collection

THESE FRIENDLY FOREST CREATURES ARE READY TO WELCOME BABY! THE WOODLAND BABIES COLLECTION INCLUDES HANGING SOFT PICTURES, A CRIB QUILT, SECURITY BLANKIE, BIB, BURP CLOTH, AND DIAPER COVER.

Woodland Babies
Soft Pictures

Finished block: 10″ × 10″

Finished pictures: 10″ × 56″

Made and quilted by
Kim Schaefer

MATERIALS

- ¼ yard of light blue for appliqué block backgrounds

- 1¼ yards total of assorted blues for borders and soft picture backs

- Scraps:

  1 rust for fox

  1 white for fox, raccoon, owl, skunk, and squirrel

  1 black for fox, raccoon, owl, skunk, and squirrel

  3 grays for raccoon and squirrel

  1 pink for fox, raccoon, skunk, and squirrel ears

  4 browns for owl

  1 orange for owl beak and talons

  2 tans for acorn

- 1¼ yards of ⅝″-wide grosgrain ribbon for hanging

- 5 squares 10½″ × 10½″ of batting

- 17 buttons (⅝″–1⅛″ size)

- 1 yard of paper-backed fusible web

- Black permanent marker for raccoon and skunk eyes

- Assorted threads for appliqué

CUTTING

Light blue

- Cut 5 squares 6½″ × 6½″ for the appliqué block backgrounds.

Assorted blues

- Cut 5 squares 10½″ × 10½″ total for the backings.

- Cut 5 rectangles 2½″ × 6½″ total for border 1.

- Cut 5 rectangles 2½″ × 8½″ total for border 2.

- Cut 5 rectangles 2½″ × 8½″ total for border 3.

- Cut 5 rectangles 2½″ × 10½″ total for border 4.

Grosgrain ribbon

- Cut 1 piece 12″ long and 8 pieces 3¾″ long.

APPLIQUÉING

Refer to Appliqué (page 7) for detailed appliqué instructions.

1. Trace and prepare the pieces for each of these woodland babies: fox, raccoon, owl, skunk, and squirrel (pages 37–41).

2. Appliqué the pieces for each woodland baby to a background square.

Block A: Fox pup

Block B: Baby raccoon

Block C: Baby owl

Block D: Baby skunk

Block E: Baby squirrel

PUTTING IT ALL TOGETHER

1. Sew the border rectangles in sequence to the appliquéd blocks. Begin with border 1 on the top edge; then add border 2 to the right edge, border 3 to the bottom edge, and end with border 4 on the left edge. Press.

2. Place and pin each bordered block right sides together with a blue backing square 10½″ × 10½″. Starting a few inches from a bottom corner, sew all the way around the perimeter, leaving an opening of about 4″ at the bottom center. Backstitch at the beginning and end.

3. Place a square of batting against the wrong side of the appliquéd block. Sew around the perimeter again, using a longer stitch and sewing within the seam allowance to secure the batting in place.

4. Trim the corners at an angle and turn each block right side out. Press. Hand stitch to close the opening.

5. Quilt-in-the-ditch along the seamlines and around the edges of the appliqué pieces. Add more quilting as desired.

FINISHING

1. Fold under each end of the 12″ piece of ribbon ½″ and press. Fold the ribbon in half. Attach the ribbon to the center of the top soft picture with a button to make the hanger.

2. Fold under each end of the 3¾″ ribbons ½″ and press. Place the ribbons ½″ from the side edges and attach the ribbons with buttons to connect the soft pictures.

29

Hoot Hoot Crib Quilt

Finished block: 6″ × 6″ • **Finished quilt:** 36½″ × 36½″

Made by Kim Schaefer, quilted by Susan Lawson of Seamingly Slawson Quilts

Sew Penguins, Puppies, Porcupines... *Oh My!*

MATERIALS

- 1¼ yards of light blue for appliqué block backgrounds and blocks
- ¾ yard of dark blue for horizontal and vertical lattice
- ¼ yard of bright for connecting squares

- Scraps for the owl body, wings, and spots:

8 pinks	4 teals
7 purples	4 greens
5 oranges	8 yellows
8 blues	8 reds

- Scraps for the owl eyes and beaks:

  1 white

  1 black

  1 orange

- 40″ × 40″ batting
- 1½ yards for backing and binding
- 2½ yards of paper-backed fusible web
- Assorted threads for appliqué

CUTTING

Light blue
- Cut 25 squares 6½″ × 6½″ for the appliqué backgrounds and blocks.

Dark blue
- Cut 60 rectangles 1½″ × 6½″ for the lattice.

Bright
- Cut 36 squares 1½″ × 1½″ for the connecting squares.

APPLIQUÉING

Refer to Appliqué (page 7) for detailed appliqué instructions.

1. Trace and prepare the pieces for 13 baby owl blocks (page 39).

2. Appliqué the baby owl pieces to the background squares.

Block A: Pink owl. Make 2.

Block B: Purple owl. Make 2.

Block C: Yellow owl. Make 2.

Block D: Orange owl. Make 1.

Block E: Blue owl. Make 2.

Block F: Teal owl. Make 1.

Block G: Green owl. Make 1.

Block H: Red owl. Make 2.

PUTTING IT ALL TOGETHER

Refer to the diagram below.

1. Arrange the blocks in 5 rows of 5 blocks each. Sew a vertical lattice rectangle between the blocks and at each end of the rows. Press.

2. Sew together 5 horizontal lattice rectangles and 6 connecting squares to make a row. Press. Make 6 rows.

3. Sew together the blocks rows and lattice rows to form the quilt top. Press.

FINISHING

1. Layer the quilt top with the batting and backing. Baste or pin.

2. Quilt as desired and bind.

Putting it all together

Baby Skunk Security Blankie

Finished blankie: 18″ × 18″

Made by
Kim Schaefer

MATERIALS

- ⅝ yard of orange minky for blankie front and back
- ½ yard of orange-and-black flannel for binding

- Scraps:
  1 black for skunk head, body, and tail
  1 white for head, body, tail, and eyes
  1 pink for ears

- ¼ yard of paper-backed fusible web
- Template plastic
- Black permanent marker for eyes
- Assorted threads for appliqué

CUTTING

Orange minky
- Cut 2 squares 18″ × 18″ for the blankie front and back.

Orange-and-black flannel
- Cut 3 bias strips 2¾″ wide for binding.

  Refer to Baby Hippo Security Blankie, Cutting, Template plastic (page 13) for the corners.

APPLIQUÉING

Refer to Appliqué (page 7) for detailed appliqué instructions.

1. Trace and prepare the pieces for the baby skunk (page 40).

2. Appliqué the baby skunk pieces to the blankie front.

3. Refer to Baby Hippo Security Blankie, Putting It All Together (page 13) to finish the blankie.

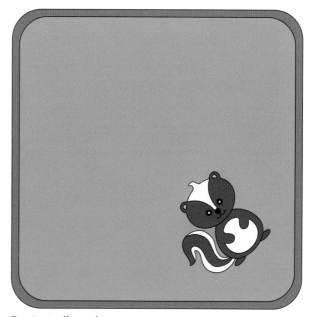

Putting it all together

Fox Pup Bib

MATERIALS

- 1 blue ready-made bib

- Scraps:

  1 red for fox body

  1 white for face, body, and tail

  1 pink for ears

  1 black for eyes, nose, and paws

- ¼ yard of paper-backed fusible web

- Assorted threads for appliqué

APPLIQUÉING

Refer to Appliqué (page 7) for detailed appliqué instructions.

1. Trace and prepare the pieces for the fox pup (page 37).

2. Appliqué the fox pup pieces to the bib.

Putting it all together

Baby Raccoon Burp Cloth

MATERIALS

• 1 ready-made burp cloth

• Scraps:

  3 grays for raccoon body, tail, tummy, and face

  1 black for nose

  1 pink for ears

  1 white for face and eyes

• ¼ yard of paper-backed fusible web

• Black permanent marker for eyes

• Assorted threads for appliqué

APPLIQUÉING

Refer to Appliqué (page 7) for detailed appliqué instructions.

1. Trace and prepare the pieces for the baby raccoon (page 38).

2. Appliqué the baby raccoon pieces to the burp cloth.

Putting it all together

Baby Skunk Diaper Cover

MATERIALS

• 1 ready-made diaper cover

• Scraps:

    1 black for skunk head, body, and tail

    1 white for head, body, tail, and eyes

    1 pink for ears

• ¼ yard of paper-backed fusible web

• Black permanent marker for eyes

• Assorted threads for appliqué

APPLIQUÉING

Refer to Appliqué (page 7) for detailed appliqué instructions.

1. Trace and prepare the pieces for the baby skunk (page 40).

2. Appliqué the baby skunk pieces to the diaper cover.

Putting it all together

Woodland Babies Patterns

FOX PUP

- Cut 1 each of pattern pieces 1–4.
- Cut 2 of pattern piece 5.
- Cut 1 and 1 reverse each of pattern pieces 6–8.

BABY RACCOON

- Cut 1 each of pattern pieces 1–9.

- Cut 1 and 1 reverse each of pattern pieces 10–13.

BABY OWL

- Cut 1 each of pattern pieces 1–5.

- Cut 2 each of pattern pieces 6–9.

- Cut 1 and 1 reverse each of pattern pieces 10 and 11.

BABY SKUNK

- Cut 1 each of pattern pieces 1–6.

- Cut 2 of pattern piece 7.

- Cut 1 and 1 reverse each of pattern piece 8.

BABY SQUIRREL

· Cut 1 each of pattern pieces 1–8.

Underwater Babies Collection

DECORATE BABY'S NURSERY WITH THIS GREAT COLLECTION OF AQUATIC BABIES. THE UNDERWATER BABIES COLLECTION FEATURES A CRIB QUILT, SECURITY BLANKIE, BIB, ONESIE, BENCH PILLOW, AND DIAPER STACKER.

Underwater Babies Crib Quilt

Finished block: 6″ × 6″ ♦ **Finished quilt:** 38½″ × 47½″

Made by Kim Schaefer, quilted by Susan Lawson of Seamingly Slawson Quilts

MATERIALS

- ½ yard of light blue for appliqué block backgrounds
- ¾ yard of medium blue for horizontal and vertical lattice strips
- ⅜ yard of dark blue for connecting squares
- ⅔ yard of multicolor stripe for outer borders

- Scraps:

  2 reds for lobster and crab

  1 peach for oyster

  3 blues for fish, whale, and whale spout

  8 greens for fish spots and fins; turtle shell, head, and tail; and frog body and tummy

  1 yellow for starfish

  1 purple for octopus

  1 teal for seahorse

  3 pinks for snail, lobster antenna, and frog tongue

  1 orange for jellyfish

  1 white for eyes

  1 black for eyes

- 42″ × 51″ batting
- 2 yards for backing and binding
- 2½ yards of paper-backed fusible web
- Black permanent marker for frog eyes
- Assorted threads for appliqué

CUTTING

Light blue

- Cut 12 squares 6½″ × 6½″ for the appliqué backgrounds.

Medium blue

- Cut 31 rectangles 3½″ × 6½″ for the lattice.

Dark blue

- Cut 20 squares 3½″ × 3½″ for the connecting squares.

Multicolor stripe

- Cut 2 strips 4½″ × 39½″ for the 2 side borders.
- Cut 2 strips 4½″ × 38½″ for the top and bottom borders.

APPLIQUÉING

Refer to Appliqué (page 7) for detailed appliqué instructions.

1. Trace and prepare the pieces for each of these underwater babies: lobster, oyster, fish, starfish, octopus, seahorse, frog, crab, whale, snail, jellyfish, and turtle (pages 52–63).

2. Appliqué the pieces for each underwater baby to a background square.

TIP: *Cut both the black and the white pieces for the eyes as whole circles. This allows you to tweak the placement of the black pupil piece, giving even more personality to these babies.*

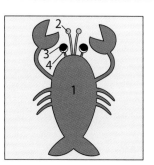

Block A: Baby lobster

Block B: Baby oyster

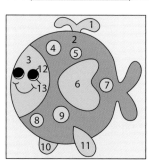

Block C: Baby fish

Block D: Baby starfish

Block E: Baby octopus

Block F: Baby seahorse

Block G: Baby frog

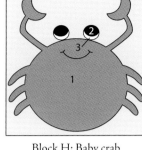

Block H: Baby crab

Block I: Baby whale

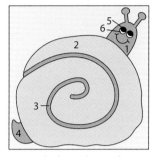

Block J: Baby snail

Block K: Baby jellyfish

Block L: Baby turtle

PUTTING IT ALL TOGETHER

Refer to the diagram below.

1. Arrange the blocks in 4 rows of 3 blocks each. Sew a vertical lattice rectangle between the blocks and at each end of the rows. Press.

2. Sew together 3 horizontal lattice rectangles and 4 connecting squares to make a row. Press. Make 5 rows.

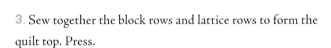

3. Sew together the block rows and lattice rows to form the quilt top. Press.

4. Sew the 2 side borders to the quilt top. Press.

5. Sew the top and bottom borders to the quilt top. Press.

FINISHING

1. Layer the quilt top with the batting and backing. Baste or pin.

2. Quilt as desired and bind.

Putting it all together

Baby Turtle Security Blankie

Finished blankie: 18″ × 18″

Made by
Kim Schaefer

MATERIALS

- ⅝ yard of green minky for blankie front and back
- ½ yard of light green flannel for binding

- Scraps:

  4 greens for turtle

  1 white for eyes

  1 black for eyes

- ½ yard of paper-backed fusible web
- Template plastic
- Assorted threads for appliqué

CUTTING

Green minky

- Cut 2 squares 18″ × 18″ for the blankie front and back.

Light green flannel

- Cut 3 bias strips 2¾″ wide for the binding.

  Refer to Baby Hippo Security Blankie, Cutting, Template plastic (page 13) for the corners.

APPLIQUÉING

Refer to Appliqué (page 7) for detailed appliqué instructions.

1. Trace and prepare the pieces for the baby turtle (page 63).

2. Appliqué the baby turtle pieces to the blankie front.

3. Refer to Baby Hippo Security Blankie, Putting It All Together (page 13) to finish the blankie.

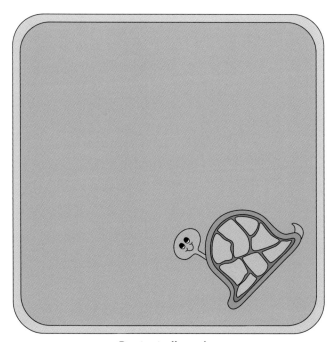

Putting it all together

Baby Starfish Bib

MATERIALS

• 1 yellow ready-made bib

• Scraps:

  1 yellow for starfish

  1 white for eyes

  1 black for eyes

• ¼ yard of paper-backed fusible web

• Assorted threads for appliqué

APPLIQUÉING

Refer to Appliqué (page 7) for detailed appliqué instructions.

1. Trace and prepare the pieces for the baby starfish (page 55).

2. Appliqué the baby starfish pieces to the bib.

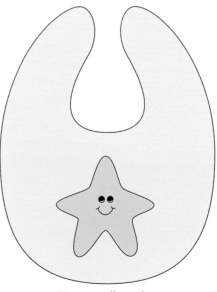

Putting it all together

Baby Crab Onesie

MATERIALS

- 1 white ready-made onesie

- Scraps:
  1 red for crab
  1 white for eyes
  1 black for eyes

- ¼ yard of paper-backed fusible web
- Assorted threads for appliqué

APPLIQUÉING

Refer to Appliqué (page 7) for detailed appliqué instructions.

1. Trace and prepare the pieces for the baby crab (page 59).

2. Appliqué the baby crab pieces to the onesie.

Putting it all together

Baby Whale Diaper Stacker

MATERIALS

- 1 blue ready-made diaper stacker

- Scraps:

  2 blues for whale and spout

  1 white for eyes

  1 black for eyes

- ¼ yard of paper-backed fusible web
- Assorted threads for appliqué

APPLIQUÉING

Refer to Appliqué (page 7) for detailed appliqué instructions.

1. Trace and prepare the pieces for the baby whale (page 60).

2. Appliqué the baby whale pieces to the diaper stacker.

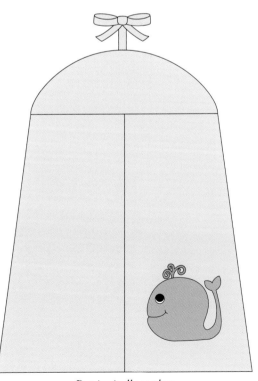

Putting it all together

Underwater Babies Bench Pillow

Finished block: 6″ × 6″ • **Finished pillow:** 24″ × 10″

Made and quilted by Kim Schaefer

MATERIALS

- ¼ yard of light blue for appliqué block backgrounds
- ⅛ yard of medium blue for lattice
- ¼ yard of dark blue for inner border
- ½ yard of multicolor stripe for outer border and pillow back

- Scraps:

  2 pinks for snail

  1 orange for jellyfish

  4 greens for turtle

  1 white for eyes

  1 black for eyes

- ½ yard of paper-backed fusible web
- Polyester fiberfill
- 2¼ yards of black piping or trim
- Assorted threads for appliqué

CUTTING

Light blue

- Cut 3 squares 6½″ × 6½″ for the appliqué backgrounds.

Medium blue

- Cut 2 rectangles 1½″ × 6½″ for the lattice.

Dark blue

- Cut 2 rectangles 1½″ × 6½″ for the side inner borders.
- Cut 2 rectangles 1½″ × 22½″ for the top and bottom inner borders.

Multicolor stripe

- Cut 2 rectangles 1½″ × 8½″ for the side outer borders.
- Cut 2 rectangles 1½″ × 24½″ for the top and bottom outer borders.
- Cut 1 rectangle 10½″ × 24½″ for the pillow back.

APPLIQUÉING

Refer to Appliqué (page 7) for detailed appliqué instructions.

1. Trace and prepare the pieces for each of these underwater babies: snail, jellyfish, and turtle (pages 61–63).

2. Appliqué the pieces for each underwater baby to a background square.

PUTTING IT ALL TOGETHER

Refer to the diagram below.

1. Arrange the appliqué blocks in a horizontal row. Sew a vertical lattice piece between the blocks. Press.

2. Sew the 2 side inner borders to the pillow front. Press.

3. Sew the top and bottom inner borders to the pillow front. Press.

4. Sew the 2 side outer borders to the pillow front. Press.

5. Sew the top and bottom outer borders to the pillow front. Press.

FINISHING

1. Pin the flat edge of the piping to the pillow front, starting at the middle of the bottom and leaving 1½″ at the end of the piping free. Pin all around, clipping at the corners.

2. Using a zipper foot, machine baste close to the cord all around. When you reach the starting point, hold the free end of the piping together and let the ends curve off the pillow edge. Stitch and trim the piping ends even with the seam allowance.

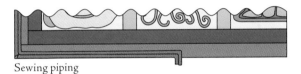

Sewing piping

3. Right sides together, sew the pillow front to the pillow back, leaving a 5″ opening at the bottom of the pillow for stuffing. Trim the seam allowance to ⅛″ at the pillow corners.

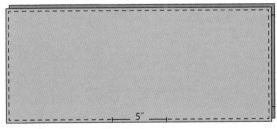

Sew pillow front to pillow back.

4. Turn the pillow right side out.

5. Stuff the pillow with polyester fiberfill.

6. Hand stitch to close the opening.

Underwater Babies Patterns

BABY LOBSTER

- Cut 1 each of pattern pieces 1 and 2.

- Cut 2 each of pattern pieces 3 and 4.

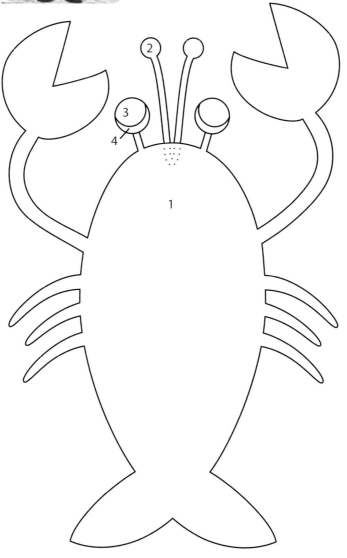

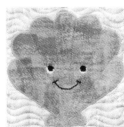

BABY OYSTER

- Cut 1 of pattern piece 1.

- Cut 2 each of pattern pieces 2 and 3.

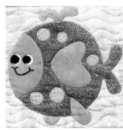

BABY FISH

- Cut 1 each of pattern pieces 1–11.

- Cut 2 each of pattern pieces 12 and 13.

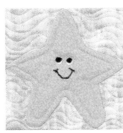

BABY STARFISH

- Cut 1 of pattern piece 1.

- Cut 2 each of pattern pieces 2 and 3.

BABY OCTOPUS

- Cut 1 of pattern piece 1.

- Cut 2 each of pattern pieces 2 and 3.

BABY SEAHORSE

· Cut 1 each of pattern pieces 1–3.

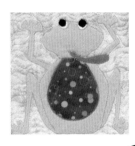

BABY FROG

- Cut 1 each of pattern pieces 1–3.

- Cut 2 each of pattern pieces 4 and 5.

BABY CRAB

· Cut 1 of pattern piece 1.

· Cut 2 each of pattern pieces 2 and 3.

BABY WHALE

· Cut 1 each of pattern pieces 1–4.

2

1

3

4

BABY SNAIL

- Cut 1 each of pattern pieces 1–4.
- Cut 2 each of pattern pieces 5 and 6.

BABY JELLYFISH

- Cut 1 each of pattern pieces 1–3.

- Cut 2 each of pattern pieces 4 and 5.

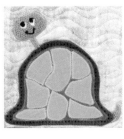

BABY TURTLE

- Cut 1 each of pattern pieces 1–12.

- Cut 2 each of pattern pieces 13 and 14.

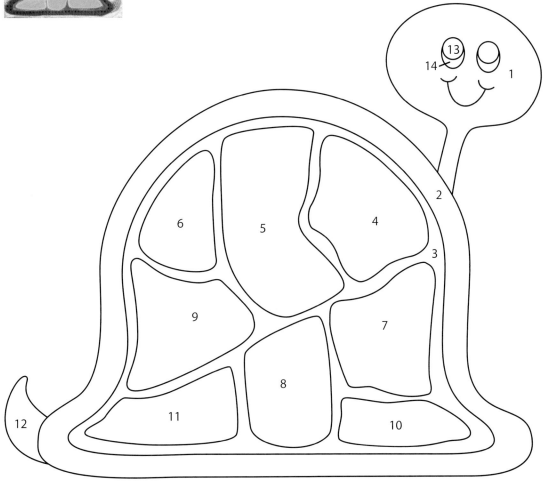

Northwoods Babies Collection

STRIKING COLORS FRAME THESE WHIMSICAL AND NOT-REALLY-WILD BABY ANIMALS. THE NORTHWOODS BABIES COLLECTION INCLUDES A CRIB QUILT, SECURITY BLANKIE, BIB, ONESIE, DIAPER COVER, AND SOFT PICTURE.

Northwoods Babies Crib Quilt

Finished block: 6″ × 6″ ◆ **Finished quilt:** 42½″ × 54½″

Made by Kim Schaefer, quilted by Susan Lawson of Seamingly Slawson Quilts

MATERIALS

- ¼ yard of gray tone-on-tone for appliqué block backgrounds
- ½ yard total of assorted reds for blocks
- 1 yard total of assorted blacks for blocks and border corners
- ⅓ yard each of light gray, dark gray, light red, and dark red for pieced border

- Scraps:

  1 white for eagle head; mountain goat body; and wolf face, tail, and paws

  1 medium brown for eagle body, bear body, porcupine body, and moose body

  1 yellow for bald eagle beak and talons

  1 tan for bear face, tummy, and paws; moose antlers and hooves; and porcupine quills

  1 dark brown for mountain goat spots and horns, and porcupine quills

  2 grays for wolf body and tail

  1 pink for mountain goat, bear, moose, porcupine, and wolf ears

  1 black for eyes, nostrils, and noses

- 46″ × 58″ batting
- 2¾ yards for backing (pieced crosswise) and binding
- 1¼ yards of paper-backed fusible web
- Assorted threads for appliqué

CUTTING

Gray tone-on-tone
- Cut 6 squares 6½″ × 6½″ for the appliqué block backgrounds.

Assorted reds
- Cut 11 squares 6½″ × 6½″ for the blocks.

Assorted blacks
- Cut 22 squares 6½″ × 6½″ for the blocks and border corners.

Light gray, dark gray, light red, and dark red
- Cut 72 rectangles 2½″ × 6½″ (18 from each ⅓ yard) for the pieced border.

APPLIQUÉING

Refer to Appliqué (page 7) for detailed appliqué instructions.

1. Trace and prepare the pieces for the Northwoods babies: bald eagle, mountain goat, bear, moose, porcupine, and wolf (pages 73–78).

2. Appliqué the pieces for each Northwoods baby to a background square.

Block A: Baby bald eagle

Block B: Baby mountain goat

Block C: Bear cub

Block D: Moose calf

Block E: Baby porcupine

Block F: Wolf pup

PUTTING IT ALL TOGETHER

Refer to the diagram below.

1. Arrange the appliqué blocks, 11 red squares, and 18 black squares in 7 rows of 5 blocks each.

2. Sew together the blocks in each row. Press.

3. Sew together the rows to form the quilt top. Press.

4. Arrange and sew together 2 sets of 21 rectangles for the 2 side borders. Press.

5. Sew the side borders to the quilt top. Press.

6. Arrange and sew together 2 sets of 15 rectangles for the top and bottom borders. Add a black corner square to each end. Press.

7. Sew the top and bottom borders to the quilt. Press.

FINISHING

1. Layer the quilt top with the batting and backing. Baste or pin.

2. Quilt as desired and bind.

Putting it all together

Bear Cub Security Blankie

Finished blankie: 18″ × 18″

Made by
Kim Schaefer

MATERIALS

- ⅝ yard of red minky for blankie front and back
- ½ yard of black-and-white flannel for binding

- Scraps:

  1 brown for bear cub head and body

  1 tan for mouth, tummy, and paws

  1 pink for ears

  1 black for eyes and nose

- ¼ yard of paper-backed fusible web
- Template plastic
- Assorted threads for appliqué

CUTTING

Red minky

- Cut 2 squares 18″ × 18″ for the blankie front and back.

Black-and-white flannel

- Cut 3 bias strips 2¾″ wide for the binding.

  Refer to Baby Hippo Security Blankie, Cutting, Template plastic (page 13) for the corners.

APPLIQUÉING

Refer to Appliqué (page 7) for detailed appliqué instructions.

1. Trace and prepare the pieces for the bear cub (page 75).

2. Appliqué the bear cub pieces to the blankie front.

3. Refer to Baby Hippo Security Blankie, Putting It All Together (page 13) to finish the blankie.

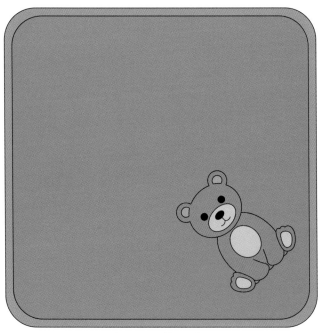

Putting it all together

Moose Calf Bib

MATERIALS

- 1 white ready-made bib

- Scraps:

  1 brown for moose calf body

  1 tan for antlers and hooves

  1 black for nostrils and eyes

  1 pink for ears

- ¼ yard of paper-backed fusible web
- Assorted threads for appliqué

APPLIQUÉING

Refer to Appliqué (page 7) for detailed appliqué instructions.

1. Trace and prepare the pieces for the moose calf (page 76).

2. Appliqué the moose calf pieces to the bib.

Putting it all together

Baby Bald Eagle Onesie

MATERIALS

- 1 gray ready-made onesie

- Scraps:

  1 brown for eagle body

  1 white for head

  1 yellow for beak and talons

  1 black for eyes

- ¼ yard of paper-backed fusible web
- Assorted threads for appliqué

APPLIQUÉING

Refer to Appliqué (page 7) for detailed appliqué instructions.

1. Trace and prepare the pieces for the baby bald eagle (page 73).

2. Appliqué the baby bald eagle pieces to the onesie.

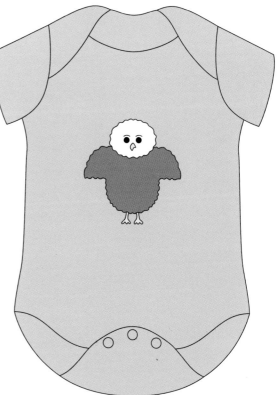

Putting it all together

Bear Cub
Diaper Cover

MATERIALS

• 1 ready-made diaper cover

• Scraps:

  1 brown for bear cub

  1 tan for mouth, tummy, and paws

  1 pink for ears

  1 black for eyes and nose

• ¼ yard of paper-backed fusible web

• Assorted threads for appliqué

APPLIQUÉING

Refer to Appliqué (page 7) for detailed appliqué instructions.

1. Trace and prepare the pieces for the bear cub (page 75).

2. Appliqué the bear cub pieces to the diaper cover.

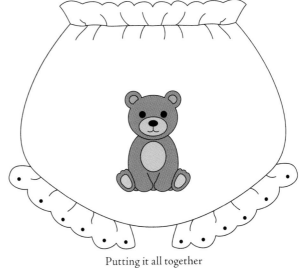

Putting it all together

Baby Porcupine Soft Picture

Finished block: 12½″ × 12½″

Made and quilted by Kim Schaefer

MATERIALS

• ¼ yard of gray for appliqué block background

• ⅛ yard total of assorted blacks for pieced border

• ⅛ yard total of assorted reds for pieced border

• Scraps:

  2 browns for porcupine body and quills

  1 tan for quills

  1 pink for ears

  1 black for nose

• 16″ × 16″ batting

• ⅔ yard for backing and binding

• ¼ yard of paper-backed fusible web

• Assorted threads for appliqué

CUTTING

Gray
• Cut 1 square 6½″ × 6½″ for the appliqué background.

Black
• Cut 18 rectangles 1½″ × 3½″ for the pieced border.

Red
• Cut 18 rectangles 1½″ × 3½″ for the pieced border.

APPLIQUÉING

Refer to Appliqué (page 7) for detailed appliqué instructions.

1. Trace and prepare the pieces for the baby porcupine (page 77).

2. Appliqué the baby porcupine pieces to the background square.

PUTTING IT ALL TOGETHER

1. Arrange and sew together 2 rows of 6 rectangles each for the 2 side borders. Press. Sew the 2 side borders to the block. Press.

2. Arrange and sew together 2 rows of 12 rectangles each for the top and bottom borders. Press. Sew the top and bottom borders to the block. Press.

FINISHING

1. Layer the quilt top with the batting and backing. Baste or pin.

2. Quilt as desired and bind.

3. Frame if desired.

Putting it all together

Northwoods Babies Patterns

BABY BALD EAGLE

- Cut 1 each of pattern pieces 1–4.

- Cut 2 of pattern piece 5.

BABY MOUNTAIN GOAT

- Cut 1 each of pattern pieces 1–13.

- Cut 2 of pattern piece 14.

- Cut 1 and 1 reverse each of pattern piece 15.

BEAR CUB

- Cut 1 each of pattern pieces 1–4.

- Cut 2 of pattern piece 5.

- Cut 1 and 1 reverse each of pattern pieces 6 and 7.

MOOSE CALF

- Cut 1 of pattern piece 1.

- Cut 2 of pattern piece 2.

- Cut 1 and 1 reverse each of pattern pieces 3–7.

BABY PORCUPINE

- Cut 1 each of pattern pieces 1–4.

- Cut 1 and 1 reverse each of pattern pieces 5 and 6.

WOLF PUP

· Cut 1 each of pattern pieces 1–9.

Farm Babies Collection

SURROUND BABY WITH FAMILIAR BARNYARD FRIENDS. THE FARM BABIES COLLECTION INCLUDES A CRIB QUILT, SECURITY BLANKIE, BURP CLOTH, DIAPER STACKER, AND TWO BIBS.

Farm Babies Crib Quilt

Finished block: *6″ × 6″* • **Finished quilt:** *48½″ × 56½″*

Made by Kim Schaefer, quilted by Susan Lawson of Seaming Slawson Quilts

MATERIALS

- ¼ yard each of 14 assorted brights for appliqué backgrounds and blocks
- 1¼ yards of medium gray for lattice, borders, and binding

- Scraps:

  1 light gold for kitten

  1 dark gold for kitten stripes

  1 white-on-white for kitten and calf

  1 black for kitten, lamb, calf, duckling eyes, and puppy nose

  2 black-on-white prints for lamb

  2 pinks for lamb, piglet, calf, mouse, and puppy

  1 yellow for duckling

  1 orange for duckling bill and feet

  2 grays for mouse

  1 white for puppy

  1 brown for puppy spots

  1 red for puppy tongue

- 52″ × 60″ batting
- 3 yards for backing (pieced crosswise)
- 1½ yards of paper-backed fusible web
- Black permanent marker for piglet, mouse, and puppy eyes
- Assorted threads for appliqué

CUTTING

Assorted brights

- Cut 56 squares 6½″ × 6½″ (4 from each ¼ yard) for the appliqué backgrounds and blocks.

Medium gray

- Cut 1 strip 2½″ × 42½″ for the lattice.

- Cut 2 strips 3½″ × 50½″ for the 2 side borders.*

- Cut 2 strips 3½″ × 48½″ for the top and bottom borders.*

Cut 6 strips 3½″ × width of fabric, piece end to end, and cut the border strips.

APPLIQUÉING

Refer to Appliqué (page 7) for detailed appliqué instructions.

1. Trace and prepare the pieces for each of these farm babies: kitten, lamb, piglet, duckling, calf, mouse, and puppy (pages 88–94).

2. Appliqué the pieces for each farm baby to a background square.

Block A: Kitten

Block B: Lamb

Block C: Piglet

Block D: Duckling

Block E: Calf

Block F: Baby mouse

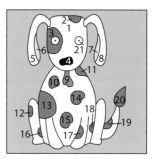

Block G: Puppy

PUTTING IT ALL TOGETHER

Refer to the diagram below.

1. Arrange the appliqué blocks in a row and sew together. Press.

2. Arrange and sew together the assorted bright squares in 7 rows of 7 blocks each. Press.

3. Sew together the rows from Step 2. Press.

4. Sew the gray lattice strip between the appliqué block row and the assorted bright rows to form the quilt top. Press.

5. Sew the 2 side borders to the quilt top. Press.

6. Sew the top and bottom borders to the quilt top. Press.

FINISHING

1. Layer the quilt top with the batting and backing. Baste or pin.

2. Quilt as desired and bind.

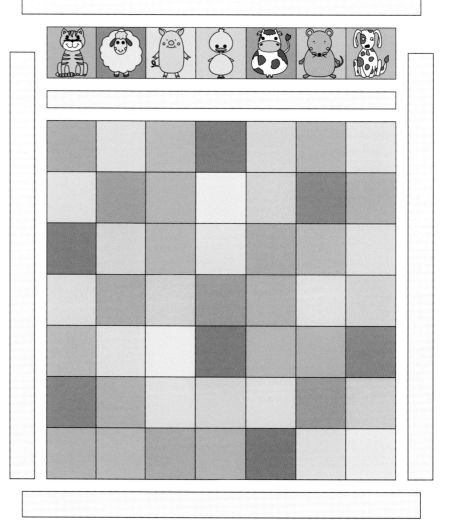

Putting it all together

Duckling Security Blankie

Finished blankie: 18″ × 18″

Made by
Kim Schaefer

- ⅝ yard of blue minky for blankie front and back
- ½ yard of yellow flannel for binding

- Scraps:

  1 yellow for duckling

  1 orange for beak and feet

  1 black for eyes

- ¼ yard of paper-backed fusible web
- Template plastic
- Assorted threads for appliqué

APPLIQUÉING

Refer to Appliqué (page 7) for detailed appliqué instructions.

1. Trace and prepare the pieces for the duckling (page 91).

2. Appliqué the duckling pieces to the blankie front.

3. Refer to Baby Hippo Security Blankie, Putting It All Together (page 13) to finish the blankie.

CUTTING

Blue minky

- Cut 2 squares 18″ × 18″ for the blankie front and back.

Yellow flannel

- Cut 3 bias strips 2¾″ wide for the binding.

  Refer to Baby Hippo Security Blankie, Cutting, Template plastic (page 13) for the corners.

Putting it all together

Calf Bib

MATERIALS

- 1 red ready-made bib

- Scraps:

   1 white for calf

   1 black for spots, tail, and eyes

   1 pink for ears and face

- ¼ yard of paper-backed fusible web
- Assorted threads for appliqué

APPLIQUÉING

Refer to Appliqué (page 7) for detailed appliqué instructions.

1. Trace and prepare the pieces for the calf (page 92).

2. Appliqué the calf pieces to the bib.

Putting it all together

Lamb Bib

MATERIALS

• 1 pink ready-made bib

• Scraps:

  2 black-on-white prints for lamb body, head, and legs

  2 pinks for face and cheeks

  1 black for ears, feet, and eyes

• ¼ yard of paper-backed fusible web

• Assorted threads for appliqué

APPLIQUÉING

Refer to Appliqué (page 7) for detailed appliqué instructions.

1. Trace and prepare the pieces for the lamb (page 89).

2. Appliqué the lamb pieces to the bib.

Putting it all together

Kitten Burp Cloth

MATERIALS

- 1 ready-made burp cloth

- Scraps:
  1 yellow for kitten
  1 gold for stripes
  1 black for eyes and whiskers
  1 white for face

- ¼ yard of paper-backed fusible web
- Assorted threads for appliqué

APPLIQUÉ

Refer to Appliqué (page 7) for detailed appliqué instructions.

1. Trace and prepare the pieces for the kitten (page 88).

2. Appliqué the kitten pieces to the burp cloth.

Putting it all together

Farm Babies Diaper Stacker

MATERIALS

· 1 pink ready-made diaper stacker

· Scraps:

2 black-on-white prints for lamb body, head, and legs

4 pinks for lamb face and cheeks; piglet; and mouse ears, cheeks, and nose

1 black for lamb eyes, ears, and feet,

2 grays for mouse

· ½ yard of paper-backed fusible web

· Black permanent marker for piglet and mouse eyes

· Assorted threads for appliqué

APPLIQUÉING

Refer to Appliqué (page 7) for detailed appliqué instructions.

1. Trace and prepare the pieces for each of these farm babies: lamb, piglet, and mouse (pages 89, 90, and 93).

2. Appliqué the pieces for each farm baby to the diaper stacker.

Putting it all together

Farm Babies Patterns

KITTEN

- Cut 1 each of pattern pieces 1–14.

- Cut 2 of pattern piece 15.

- Cut 1 and 1 reverse each of pattern pieces 16–19.

LAMB

· Cut 1 each of pattern pieces 1–11.

· Cut 2 of pattern piece 12.

PIGLET

· Cut 1 each of pattern pieces 1 and 2.

· Cut 2 of pattern piece 3.

· Cut 1 and 1 reverse each of pattern pieces 4–6.

DUCKLING

· Cut 1 each of pattern pieces 1–3.

· Cut 2 of pattern piece 4.

CALF

- Cut 1 each of pattern pieces 1–10.

- Cut 2 of pattern piece 11.

- Cut 1 and 1 reverse each of pattern pieces 12–14.

BABY MOUSE

- Cut 1 each of pattern pieces 1–3.

- Cut 2 of pattern piece 4.

- Cut 1 and 1 reverse each of pattern pieces 5–7.

PUPPY

- Cut 1 each of pattern pieces 1–20.

- Cut 2 of pattern piece 21.

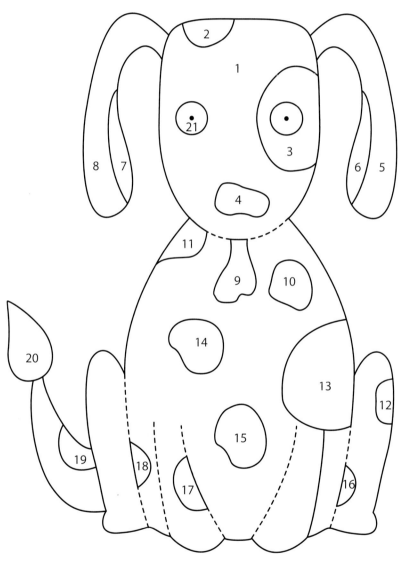

About the Author

KIM SCHAEFER began sewing at an early age and was quilting seriously by the late 1980s. Her early quilting career included designing and producing small quilts for craft shows and shops across the country.

In 1996, Kim founded Little Quilt Company, a pattern company focused on designing a variety of small, fun-to-make projects.

In addition to designing quilt patterns, Kim is a best-selling author for C&T Publishing. Kim also designs fabric for Andover Fabrics.

Kim lives with her family in Southeastern Wisconsin.

Photo by Rick Swearingen, Mortensen Photography

Visit Kim online and follow on social media!

WEBSITE:

littlequiltcompany.com

See Kim's entire collection of patterns, books, and fabrics!

FACEBOOK:

Little Quilt Company

See posts about new patterns, books, and fabrics and an occasional peek at Kim's latest work!

ALSO BY KIM SCHAEFER

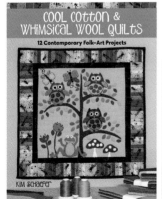